My Book of

REPTILES

Written by
Zunairah Rafay
&
Sufia Nasir

Watch this book come to life
in the **lambkinz**™ app
where books come to life

Download now on

or watch exclusively on
watch.lambkinz.com

Have you ever wondered what Reptiles are like?

For instance, why do we **fear** some of these interesting creatures?

Or what are the factors that make them so special?

Let's learn about the amazing qualities that make Reptiles so unique.

Reptiles are cold blooded creatures.

They lay eggs and their skin is coated with dry hard scales.

They need heat from their surroundings to warm up themselves.

Reptiles often crawl on their bellies. Most of them have tiny short legs.

Reptiles tend to live in mild and tropical climates.

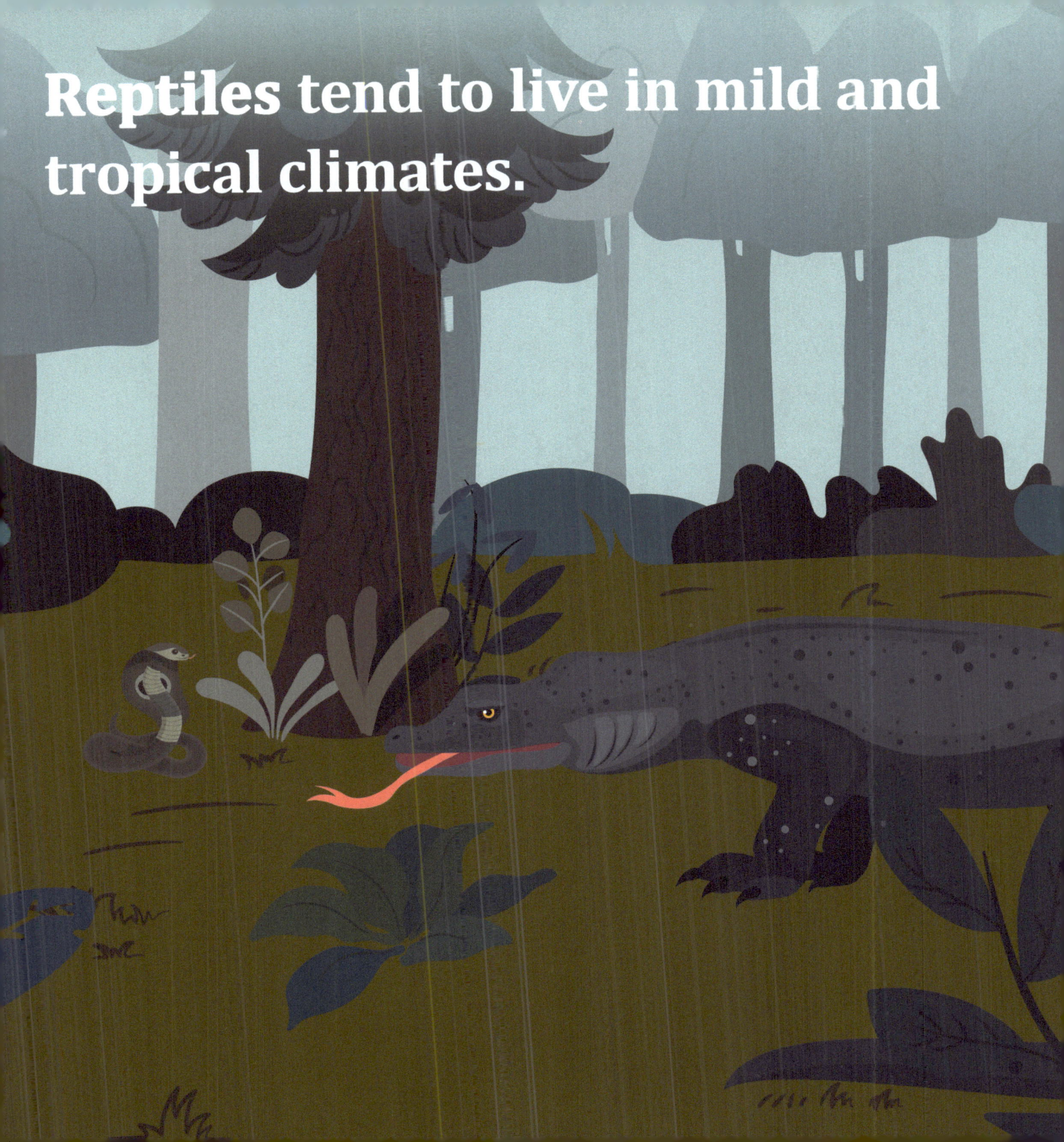

All Reptiles have a backbone or spine, which means they are vertebrates.

Its now time to explore some reptiles.

Alligators and Crocodiles

Alligators and Crocodiles have existed for millions of years.

They eat other creatures such as fish, birds, turtles and even deer.

The coolest thing is that they can see well at night.

Alligators and Crocodiles have a great vision underwater.

Here is what they look like:

Alligators have broad U-shaped snouts.

Crocodiles have front ends that are more pointed and V-shaped.

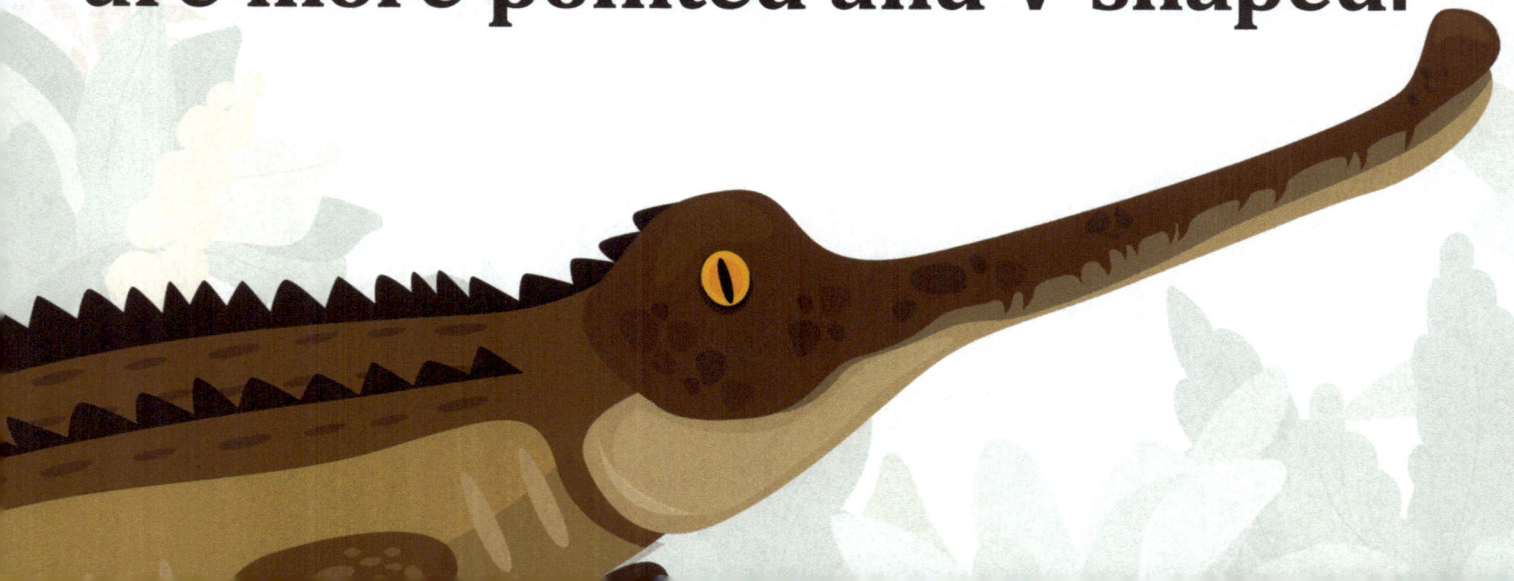

Snakes

Snakes live around all the continents of the world except for Antarctica.

They have very flexible jaws.

Their jaws allow them to swallow larger prey.

Snakes eat eggs, birds, ants, frogs,
lizards and other snakes.

Some examples are

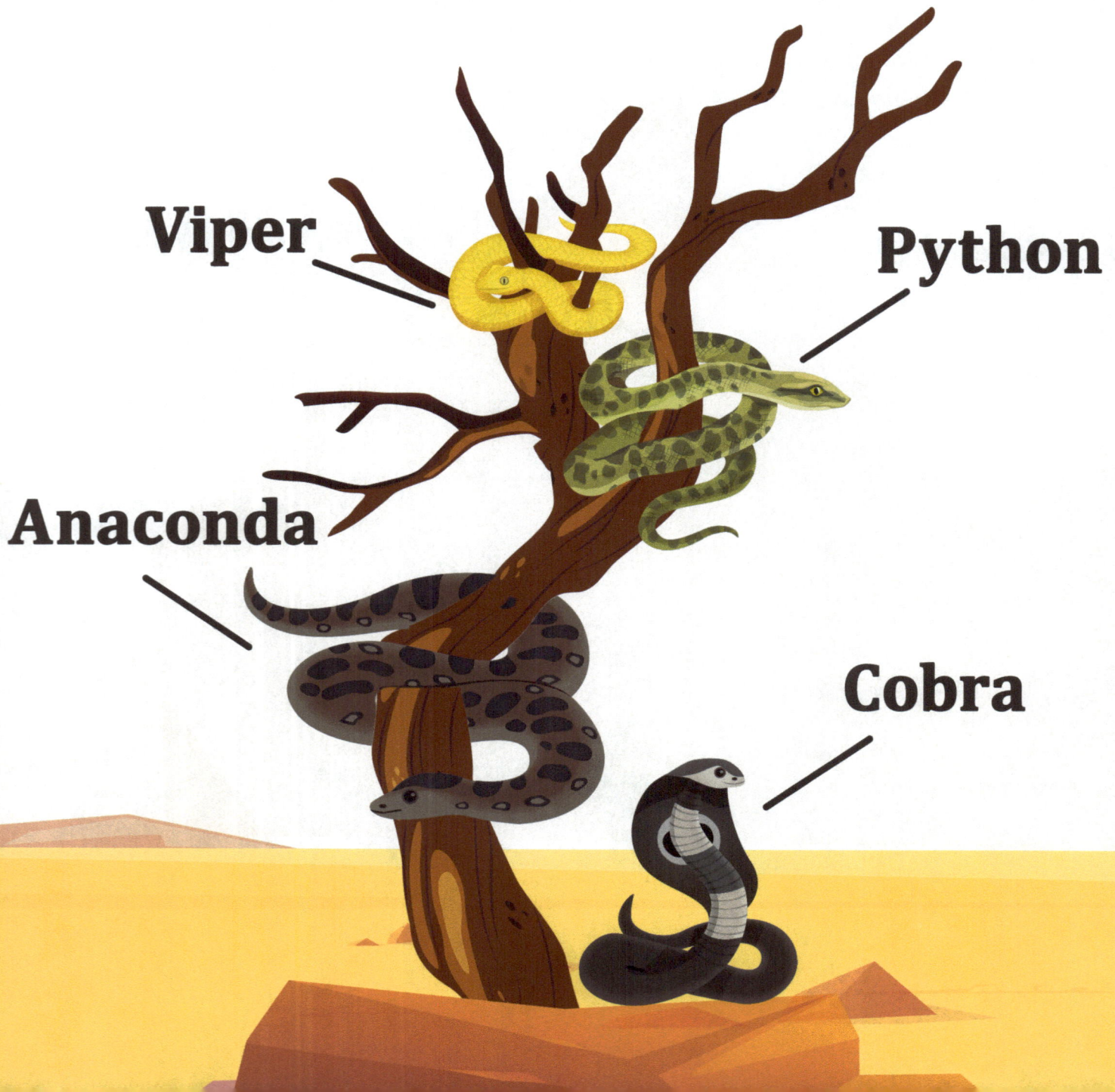

Viper

Python

Anaconda

Cobra

Turtles and Tortoises

Turtles and Tortoises belong to the oldest reptile groups of the world.

Their shell is a shield to protect them from other predators.

When in need of protection, some turtles tuck their head inside their shell.

They eat beetles, fish, fruit and grass.

They have a long life span.

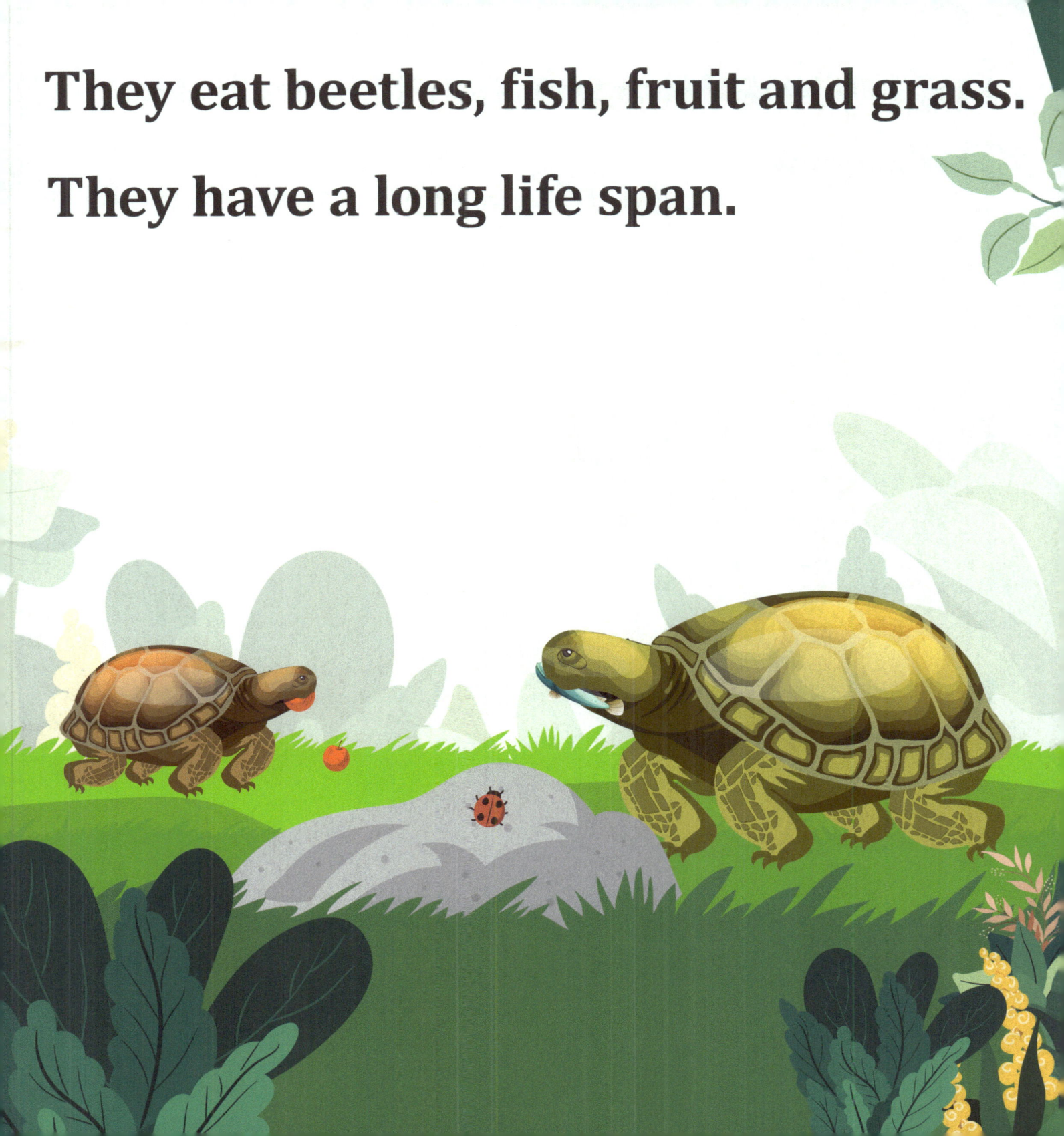

Tortoises live on the land while Turtles live in the water.

Lizards

Lizards are found almost all over the world.

They have scales for skin,
a long body, a pointy tail, and
usually four legs.

Lizards can be smaller than an inch long or massive in size and weight.

They eat ants, spiders and termites.

Chameleons

Chameleons are a type of lizard.

They have very long tongues.

Chameleons can even change colour.
This is called camouflaging.

Geckos

Geckos are usually small with soft skin.

They also have a short, stout body with a large head.

They have unique toes which make them excellent climbers.

Iguanas

Iguanas are very interesting creatures.

They usually have saggy skin on their throats.

Iguanas are popular pets and can live for up to 20 years.

Iguanas can punch their enemies with their tail.

Komodo Dragon

Komodo dragons are the heaviest lizards on Earth.

They have long, flat heads with rounded snouts, scaly skin, bowed legs and huge muscular tails.

They are meat eaters and can be very, very aggressive.

That's why they are known as Komodo Dragons.

Most **Reptiles** can survive for a long time without food.

But when they eat, they eat insects, mollusks, fish, birds, frogs & mammals.

Now that you know everything about eccentric Reptiles,

which one is your favourite kind?

Explore more titles

ننھی پیرو
ارفع کریم
مرتب کردہ: لیکینز

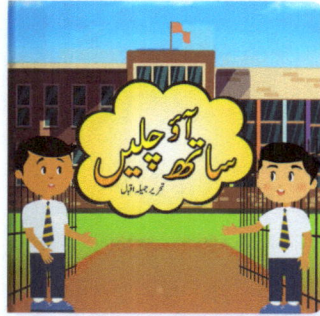

ساتھ آؤ چلیں
تحریر: چاند اقبال

حضرت یوسف
اور بادشاہ کا خواب
مرتب کردہ: لیکینز

حضرت یونس
اور مچھلی

پیاری باتیں
دو اہم الفاظ
تحریر
ناصر حسین

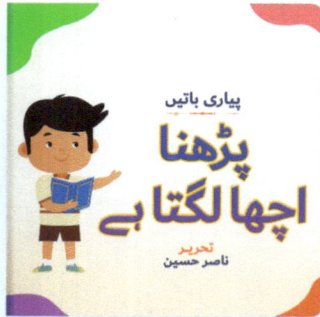

پیاری باتیں
پڑھنا اچھا لگتا ہے
تحریر
ناصر حسین

پیاری باتیں
ہماری ٹیچر
تحریر
ناصر حسین

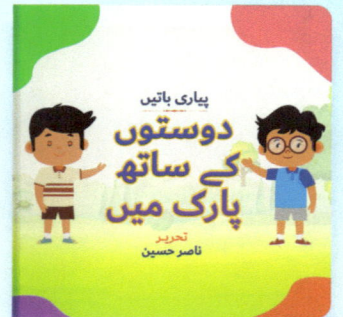

پیاری باتیں
دوستوں کے ساتھ پارک میں
تحریر
ناصر حسین

عید مبارک
تحریر صوفیہ ناصر

بقر عید مبارک
تحریر صوفیہ ناصر

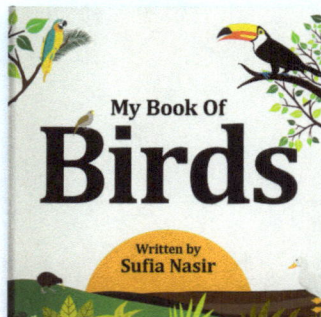

My Book Of
Birds
Written by
Sufia Nasir

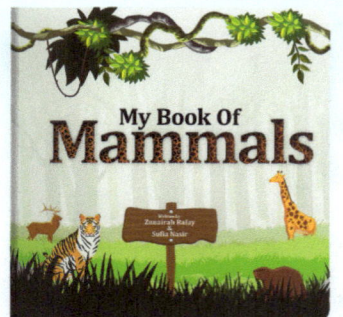

My Book Of
Mammals

Watch all our books come to life with playful animation, gentle music & lifelike sound effects in the lambkinz app

lambkinz™
where books come to life

lambkinz combines the joy of reading storybooks with playful animation. lambkinz features dozens of gorgeous original stories, general knowledge & instructionals for kids to enjoy & learn from.

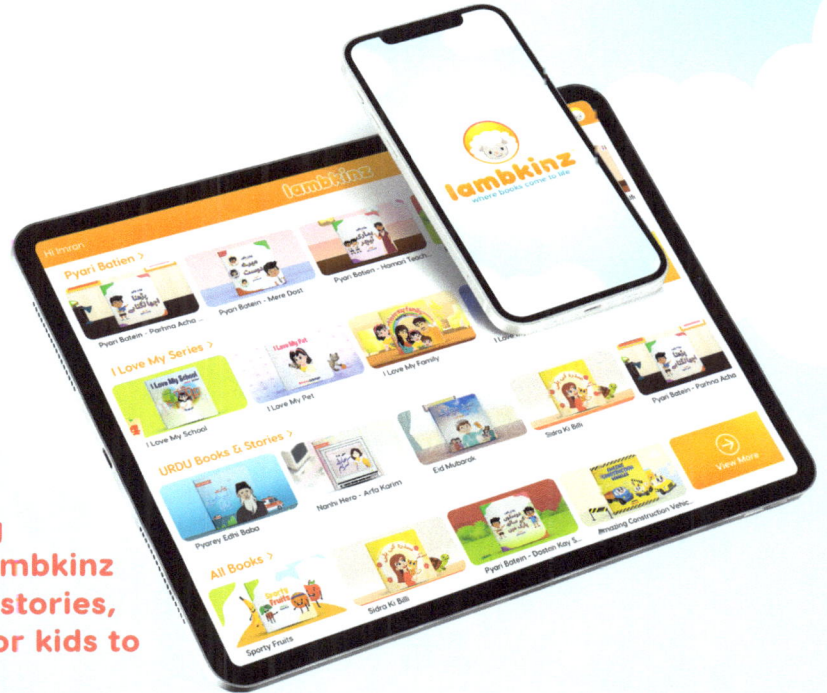

Download the **lambkinz** app for your device.

Download on the App Store

GET IT ON Google Play

lambkinz is a registered trademark of Green Animation Studio™

www.ingramcontent.com/pod-product-compliance
Lightning Source LLC
Chambersburg PA
CBHW061136030426
42334CB00003B/64